Learn Spanish

A beginner's guide to learning basic Spanish fast, including useful common words and phrases!

Table Of Contents

Introduction 1

Chapter 1: Why Learn Spanish 2

Chapter 2: The Spanish Alphabet 5

Chapter 3: Everything about Nouns in Spanish 8

Chapter 4: A Little Bit of Spanish Vocabulary 13

Chapter 5: Everything about Pronouns 26

Chapter 6: Verbs in Spanish 28

Conclusion 34

Introduction

I want to thank you and congratulate you for downloading the book, "Learn Spanish".

This book contains helpful information about how you can learn the basics of Spanish fast! It is not an all-inclusive and exhaustive book on the Spanish language. However, it will teach you enough of the very basics to help you learn rudiments of the language on your own.

Without making any insane claims of being able to teach you the entire Spanish language within hours, this book will still be of great assistance. It has the information required to teach you the fundamentals of Spanish, and how the language is spoken.

This includes the fundamental words, sayings, and expressions that you need to conduct simple conversations. This also involves correct pronunciation, sentence structure, and the masculine/feminine versions of words. You will learn about the different pronouns, nouns, adjectives, and verbs, and when to use each.

This book is a perfect guide for beginners, and will explain to you tips and techniques that will allow you to begin successfully speaking basic Spanish in no time! The fundamentals in this book will keep you busy for some time, and will make learning the entire language a simple and smooth process!

Thanks again for downloading this book, I hope you enjoy it!

Chapter 1:
Why Learn Spanish

Some people say that Spanish is a romantic language. Well, if you really want to speak to your Spanish speaking head-turner next door neighbor, then by all means, learn the language. Other than that, there are actually a lot of other reasons why people should learn how to speak the language.

Making Yourself Marketable

There are plenty of jobs out there that will require a professional to speak Spanish. It is actually the second most spoken language in the entire United States of America. Some experts also say that it is one of the fastest growing languages in the nation. How does learning a second language, particularly Spanish, make you more marketable?

Remember that the world is now bent on globalization. Companies are broadening their markets. That means you should be able to interact with clients and partners from another country. If you speak Spanish then that makes you better equipped for interacting with people from Spanish speaking countries. Many employers usually feel inclined to hire bilingual employees nowadays. This is true in various fields and careers, including but not limited to; customer service, social services, healthcare, and even in education.

The Second Biggest Spanish Speaking Country

Believe it or not, the US is the second biggest Spanish speaking nation in the world. There are 50 million Spanish speaking people in the United States alone. The number one country is Mexico. That also means there are more Spanish speaking Americans than there native Spanish speakers in Spain itself.

If your company is trying to reach new markets, then 50 million people is a pretty big niche.

Expanding your horizons to the rest of the world, you will be reaching out to more than 350 million Spanish speakers globally. You'll be able to interact well with many South American countries and other countries in growing markets in the pacific. That is about one third of a billion people worldwide.

It's Really Easy to Learn

Studies show that Spanish is one of the easiest languages to learn by native English speakers. The grammar structures of both English and Spanish are a bit similar. The cultural contexts are also alike in many ways.

It's Rooted in History

There are many countries that have felt the influence of Spain throughout the world. Even in the United States, you will find many places that actually have Spanish names. If the name of a town, state, or country is Spanish, chances are that place has some sort of history with Spain and its language.

It Makes Your Travel Experience Much Better

Having language barriers on a road trip is a big spoiler for many vacations. How many times have you experienced not understanding what the locals are saying? It's such a wonderful experience to be able to talk to local Spanish speakers and know exactly what to say to them.

Learn Another Language Much Easier

It is often claimed by people who have learned Spanish as their second language that they have learned a third language much easier. The ordeal of learning new words, practicing, and speaking, is a life skill. Once you know the rudiments, learning a third or even a fourth language is made a somewhat effortless. By that time you will be able to easily spot common elements across different languages.

Chapter 2:
The Spanish Alphabet

The good thing about the Spanish language is that the characters of the alphabet are very similar to English. That means native English speakers won't need to learn any new symbols. That means you need less time to learn how to speak Spanish. Now, here are the letters of the Spanish alphabet:

a, b, c, ch, d, e, f, g, h, i, j, k, l, ll, m, n, ñ, o, p, q, r, rr, s, t, u, v, w, x, y, z

This alphabet somewhat looks like the usual English alphabet that you learned in school, right? There are only a few minor additions. You won't think that "ch" should be a letter but it is considered as such in Spanish. The other additional characters include ll, ñ, and rr. The order of the letters also looks very much like the order you learned the English alphabet as well, which makes it really easy to memorize.

Pronouncing the Spanish Letters

Becoming familiar with the letters used in Spanish isn't the first big challenge. It's learning how to pronounce them that will prove to be a bit difficult. It should be obvious that even though two languages use the same letters or characters, it doesn't mean that the letters are pronounced in exactly the same way.

The following list details how each letter in the Spanish alphabet is pronounced:

- a = "ah" as in "far"

- e = "ay" as in "day." But it is also pronounced as "eh" as in "bed"

- i = "ee" as in "see"
- = "oh" as in "told"
- u = "oo" as in "boot"
- c = "k" in "keep"
- c = is also pronounced as "s" as in "cider"
- c = is also pronounced as "ks" as in "accept"
- ch = "ch" as in "church"
- g = "g" as in "good" if it is used before the vowels a, o, and u.
- g = is also pronounced as "h" as in "hello" when the "g" is placed before an "e" or an "i"
- j = is pronounced as "h" as in "hat"
- l = "l" as in "leap"
- ll = "y" as in "yellow"
- n = "n" as in "north"
- ñ = combines the sound of n+y "ny" as in "ca**ny**on"
- qu = "k" as in "key"
- r = "r" just like the way it is pronounced in English with a trill
- rr = "rr" you should pronounce this letter with a strong trill

- s = "s" just like the way it is pronounced in English
- v = this is pronounced like a soft "b" in English
- x = if this letter appears before a consonant then you pronounce it "see"
- x = if this letter appears before a vowel then you pronounce it as "ks" as in "boo**ks**"
- y = if this letter is found within a word then pronounce it as an "e" as in "yet"
- y = if this letter is alone then pronounce it as in "see"
- z = "s" as in "sat"

Tip: If you are experiencing some sort of difficulty trying to pronounce some of the unique Spanish sounds, it will be very helpful to find someone who does speak Spanish and ask them to pronounce it for you. You can practice afterwards. You can also listen to some free audio online or watch how they say it in actual Spanish on TV. It may be a bit challenging at first but with some practice you'll get the hang of it.

Chapter 3:
Everything about Nouns in Spanish

In this chapter we'll dive right into the Spanish language and talk about nouns. We all know that nouns are the words we basically use to denote an idea, a thing, a place, or a person. That's the easy part. The difficulty lies in the fact that nouns in Spanish are either masculine (male) or feminine (female). That can sound like a pretty odd concept but it is true not only in Spanish but also in other languages in the world like Greek for example.

Denoting Gender in Nouns

The good news is that figuring out which nouns are masculine and which ones are feminine is fairly easy in Spanish. One way to help you out is to look for the definite articles "el" and "la." You will use "el" for masculine and "la" for feminine.

Examples of this concept:

    el chico = masculine, it translates to "boy"

    la chica = feminine, it translates to "girl"

    el jardin = masculine, it translates to "garden"

    la universidad = feminine, it translates to "university"

    el libro = masculine, it translates to "book"

    la revista = feminine, it translates to "magazine"

    el miedo = masculine, it translates to "fear"

    la libertad = feminine, it translates to "liberty"

This shouldn't be a difficult concept to understand. It also appears to some degree in English as well. For instance, when referring to liberty, you sometimes will call it "lady liberty." The only difficulty here is that even non-living objects are designated masculine and feminine genders. English speakers usually think in terms of male and female persons where gender is concerned.

In the examples provided here, you will also notice that when a word ends in "o" the noun is given a masculine gender, whether you're talking about a living thing or not. When the noun ends in "a" then the noun usually receives a female gender. That is the case with "chico" (male) and "chica" (female). However, you should note that there are exceptions to this rule.

It is also easy to deduce that the definite articles "el" and "la" actually mean the same thing. They can be translated to "the" in English. They mean the same thing but they serve as markers for gender. Thus "el chico" is translated as "the boy" and "la chica" is translated as "the girl."

Denoting Gender in Non-Living Things

The difficulty with denoting the masculinity of objects and other non-living things is that there is no hard and fast rule about it. Sometimes you may think that a Spanish noun is masculine simply because it is designated for males in English. Such is not the case.

For example:

You usually say "la corbata" (the necktie). If you think in English terms, a necktie should be worn by men thus some may make that association and say "el corbata." But the correct way to say it is "la corbata" (feminine).

Now here's another example. Try to think which definite article you're supposed to use for "vestido" (dress). If you associate the word "dress" with a woman in English then you will be mistaken. It's supposed to be "el vestido" (masculine).

As stated earlier, there are no hard and fast rules to go about it. You may think that you should check whether the noun ends in "o" or "a" but you'll soon find out that this isn't always the case. Some masculine nouns end in "a" and some feminine nouns end in "o." The best approach is to learn new nouns and then immediately associate the right definite article that goes with it.

A Few Clues

Masculine nouns may also end in l, n, and r. The days of the week are masculine. The things that you can see in nature are usually masculine. The names of months are also masculine. Spanish words with Greek origin are also masculine – the ones that end in ta, pa, or ma.

Feminine words may also end in ie, umbre, ez, sion, cion, tud, tad, and dad. The names of cities as well as towns also take on a feminine gender. So, you may ask why all the fuss about masculine and feminine nouns? The Spanish language puts a huge emphasis on it, which isn't that evident in English.

Plural Forms

If you find a noun that ends in a vowel, you will form its plural by adding an "s" at the end. For example:

    chico (singular); chicos (plural)

    señora (singular); señoras (plural)

Note that the definite article that goes with a noun also changes when the noun takes on a plural form. The article "el" becomes "los" and the article "la" becomes "las" as in the following examples:

    el chico (singular); los chicos (plural)

    la pluma (singular); las plumas (plural)

If you find a noun that ends in a consonant, you will make its plural form by adding "es."

Examples:

    el professor will become ***los profesores***

    la universidad will become ***las universidades***

You will also find nouns that end in "ion" and they will also have a written accent. You form its plural by adding "es" and dropping the accent marks.

Example:

    la televisión forms its plural as ***las televisions***

Note: the accent on ó was dropped

Some nouns end in "z," form its plural by changing z to c and then you add "es."

Example:

el tapiz forms its plural as *los tapices*

Some nouns form their plural by making compound nouns. Note that these compound nouns always take on a masculine gender.

Example:

abre (open) and lata (can) may combine into abrelatas (literally translates to "open cans") but the new word actually means "can opener." And since it takes on a masculine form then you say el abrelatas (singular) and los abrelatas (to denote plural).

One Final Plural and Gender Rule

There are times when a noun will refer to a group and that group will have members from different genders (like male and female students etc.). In such a case, your noun will take on a plural form.

Example:

A group has 5 gato as well as 5 gatas. You will still say you have 10 gatos. Use the male plural form of the noun instead of the female.

Chapter 4:
A Little Bit of Spanish Vocabulary

After learning the Spanish alphabet, the next step is to learn a few words in Spanish. You won't understand the rest of the instructions in the chapters that follow if you don't work on your vocabulary. We'll begin with a few terms that even children get to learn when they study the language for the first time.

Days of the Week

Let's start by learning the days of the week first. This will be good practice in your study of nouns and other words. It will also help reinforce what you have already learned so far. The days in Spanish are as follows:

Monday = *lunes*

Tuesday = *martes*

Wednesday = *miércoles*

Thursday = *jueves*

Friday = *viernes*

Saturday = *sábado*

Sunday = *domingo*

Note that in many Spanish speaking countries they begin their week with Monday and not Sunday. Another thing that you should notice is that in Spanish you don't need to capitalize the first letter of the names of each day. Since all days of the week in Spanish are masculine you mention them as such:

el lunes

el martes

el miércoles

el jueves

el viernes

el sábado

el domingo

Note that definite articles change in meaning when they are used in conjunction with the days of the week. In this case, they are used to denote time like in the English preposition "on" for example "on Monday." Consider the following example:

No trabajo el jueves. (I don't work on Thursday)

Another peculiar thing about the days of the week in Spanish is the fact that the names that end in "es" don't change when you form its plural. That means they just use the definite article used for plural nouns but don't really change in form:

- **el lunes** when changed to plural is just **los lunes**
- **el martes** when changed to plural is just **los martes**
- **el miércoles** when changed to plural is just **los miércoles**
- **el jueves** when changed to plural is just **los jueves**
- **el viernes** when changed to plural is just **los viernes**

- ***el sábado*** when changed to plural is just ***los sábados***
- ***el domingo*** when changed to plural is just ***los domingos***

If you want to say what day it is, you will use the verb "es" to denote the actual day. Consider the following example:

Hoy es martes translates to ***Today is Tuesday***.

You also use the same verb when you ask what day it is; just like in the following example:

You say ***Qué día es hoy?*** That translates to "What day is today?"

To indicate the future or the near future, you will have to use the indicative of the present tense. Consider the following example:

- When you say "***Salimos el lunes***" you are actually saying either "We leave on Monday" or "We will leave on Monday."

Counting 1 to 10 in Spanish

Counting is also an integral part of any new language you will learn. We'll start with the very basics. Here are the numbers 1 to 10 in Spanish in ascending order:

Un

dos

tres

cuatro

cinco

seis

siete

ocho

nueve

diez

The numbers in Spanish also change and transform when they relate to different words in a sentence. Here are a few rules that you ought to know.

- "uno" (i.e. the number 1) changes to "un" when is positioned before a noun that is masculine. For instance: "un libro" (one book).

- If "uno" is placed before a noun that is feminine then it changes to "una." For instance: "una chica" (one girl).

- When you're counting along and are just mentioning numbers then you just say the numbers in their original forms, like uno, dos, tres, cuatro, cinco, etc. That means you will be saying "uno" instead of "un"

- However, if you're counting specific things, "uno" will change to "un." For instance "un libro" (if masculine) or "una pluma" (if feminine).

More Samples of Nouns in Spanish

Gente: people

Tipo: type, kind

Fin: end

Manera: way or manner

Mano: hand

Punto: point, period, dot

Trabajo: work, effort, job

Hora: time or hour

Persona: person

Lugar: position or place

País: country

Caso: occasion or case

Mujer: wife or woman

Mundo: world

Casa: house

Forma: form, way, or shape

Momento: time or moment

Vida: life

Parte: portion or part

Hombre: mankind, man, or husband

Cosa: thing

Día: day

Tiempo: weather or time (as in timing)

Año: year

Vez: time (pertaining to the number of times)

Samples of Adjectives in Spanish

Su: his, her, their, your

Poco: little, few; a little bit

Lo: the (+ neuter)

Tanto: so much, so many

Todo: all, every

Nuestro: our

Más: more

Cada: each, every

Este: this

Menos: less, fewer

Otro: other, another

Nuevo: new

Samples of Prepositions in Spanish

De: of, from

Desde: from, since

A: to, at

Hacia: toward

En: in

Contra: against, opposite

Por: for, by, through

Bajo: under, underneath

Con: with

Ante: before, in the presence of

Para: for, to, in order to

Según: according to

Sin: without

Tras: after, behind

Sobre: on top of, over, about

Mediante: by means of

Hasta: until, up to, even (adverb)

Except: except (for)

Entre: between, among

Samples of Spanish Verbs and Phrases

The following are some common and useful Spanish verbs and other phrases that you should get to know. Some of them are the ones that we will be using in the next few chapters as examples:

venir: to come

tener: to have

estar: to be

llegar: to arrive

pasar: to pass, spend time

ser: to be

vivir: to live

llevar: to take, carry

comer: to eat

hablar: to speak

llamar: to call, name

hay: there are/there is

saber: to find out

si: yes

no: no

por favor: please

gracia: thank you

no se: I don't know

en que: in which

despacio: slow down

viajero: traveler

salida: exit

entrada: entrance

lo siento: sorry

no gracias: no, thank you

de nada: you're welcome

perdone la molestia : I'm sorry to bother you

puede decírme?: Can you tell me?

dónde está...?:   where is...?

dónde está el baño?: Where is the bathroom?

¿Que desea?: What do you want?

Quiero: I want/ would like

a que distancia?: How far?

cuánto cuesta?: How much does it cost?

cómo?: How?

dónde?: Where?

¿qué?: What?

¿por qué?: Why?

¿quién?: Who?

¿Cuándo?: When?

Some Useful Greetings in Spanish

Buenas noches: Good Night

Bienvenido: Welcome

Hola: Hello

Buenas tardes: Good Afternoon or Good Evening

Hasta luego: See you later

Buenos días: Good Day or Good Morning

Hasta pronto: See you soon

Adios: Good-bye

Hasta mañana: See you tomorrow

Some Useful Phrases When Greeting People

¿Cómo se llama usted?: What is your name? (formal way of saying it)

Yo trabajo en...: I work in...

¿Cómo te llamas?: What is your name? (informal way of saying it)

¿Cúal es tu nombre?: What is your name?

Dejame presentarte a...: Let me introduce you to...

¿Cómo es tu apellido?: What is your last name?

Mucho gusto: Very nice to meet you.

Un gusto conocerlo: Nice to meet you (the formal way of saying it)

Ésto es...: This is...

Un gusto conocerte: Nice to meet you. (the informal way of saying it)

¿A qué te dedicas?: What do you do for a living?

Some Spanish phrases you can use for shopping:

Busco: I am looking for

Una tienda de ropa: A clothing store

Una farmacia: A pharmacy

Una panaderia: A bakery

Un almacén: A department store

Más grande: Larger

No me gusta.: I do not like it.

Una libreria: A bookstore

¿Cuánto es?: How much is it?

Más pequeño: Smaller

¡Por favor muéstreme!: Please show me

Aqui está: Here it is

Dónde se puede encontrar...: Where can I find...

Más barato: Cheaper

Necesito un intérprete: I need an interpreter

¿Hay alguien aqui que hable ingles?: Does anyone here speak English?

Mejor: Better

Una tienda de comestibles: A grocery store

¡Fantástico ¿Cuál es el precio?: Great how much is it?

Spanish Phrases When You're Out to Eat

¡Señorita!: Miss!

Señor: Mister

Tengo hambre: I am hungry

Tengo sed: I am thirsty

Tenemos hambre: We are hungry

Tenemos sed: We are thirsty

Quisiera hacer una reserva: I would like to make a reservation

Tengo una reserve: I have a reservation

¿Hay platos speciales para los niños?: Do you have children's portions?

¿Hay una carta para los niños?: Do you have a children's menu?

Café con crema: Coffee with cream

Café con azúcar: Coffee with sugar

Café: Coffee

Chapter 5:
Everything about Pronouns

In this chapter we'll dive into pronouns in Spanish. Pronouns are used as substitute for nouns in a sentence. Subject pronouns such as they, we, she, he, you, and I take on the following forms in Spanish:

I = yo

they = ellos

you = usted

you-all = ustede

he = él

we = nosotros

she = ella

The subject pronouns in Spanish have similar characteristics to their English counterparts. However, it is also important to note their differences. As an example, in the list mentioned above, the pronoun "you" is translated in Spanish as "usted." However, there is a second way to translate it, which is tú. The formal way of saying you in Spanish is "usted" while the informal way of saying it is "tú."

So, when you're speaking to your boss or an authority higher than you, then use "usted." But when you're speaking to your son you use "tú." If you're talking to your teacher you should use "usted." However, when speaking to an acquaintance use "tú."

The plural form of this pronoun also has a formal and informal application. For instance, when you are addressing a crowd while giving a speech you use the plural form ustedes. On the other hand, when you're announcing something to a group of friends in a bar you should use the less formal pronoun "vosotros."

Masculine and Feminine Pronouns

Since Spanish emphasizes gender more than English does, you should already expect that pronouns require a masculine or a feminine form as well. In the previous example above, you basically say nosotros when referring to a group of males (or a mixed group with both males and females in it). But you will use nosotras when referring to an all-female group.

The same is true for the Spanish word for "they." You say ellos for a bunch of boys (or a mixed group of boys and girls). But you say ellas only to a group of girls.

Vosotros is used for a group of guys (or a mixed group of guys and girls). Vosotras on the other hand is used for a group that consists of girls only. On another note, remember that these forms are more familiar to Spain and may not be as familiar to our Latin American folks who also speak Spanish.

Chapter 6:
Verbs in Spanish

In this next chapter we will look into the verbs in the Spanish language. We'll begin with one of the most curious verbs in the language – "hay." This verb actually takes on a couple of meanings. The first meaning is that of the presence of one object. The other meaning refers to the presence of more than one or multiple objects.

Here's an example of the singular:

Hay un libro. (There is a book)

Hay una pluma. (There is a pen)

Here's an example of the plural:

Hay muchos libros en la biblioteca. (There are many books in the library)

The verb "hay" can mean "there is" and also "there are." Note that it needs an identifier for you to determine whether it is singular or plural. The following illustrates how "hay" takes on plural meanings:

Hay cuatro (there are four)

Hay dos (there are two)

Hay muchos (there are many)

The same is true when "hay" is used to ask questions. It also needs another word to help define whether it is singular or plural. Observe the following examples.

Hay un biblioteca?

(Is there a library?)

Hay muchos chicas?

(Are there lots of girls?)

It should also be noted that you can use "hay" to answer questions. Note the following examples:

No. No hay. (No. No there aren't)

Sí. Sí hay. (Yes. Yes there is)

Regular and Irregular Verbs

It should be noted here that all verbs in Spanish are either regular verbs or irregular verbs. Remember the three different verb endings below. They will be very common as you learn more verbs in this language.

-ar verbs (e.g. hablar)

-ir verbs (e.g. vivir)

-er verbs (e.g. comer)

The verb groups above are the three verb categories you will find in Spanish. Note that all three verb categories will have infitives or what is known as their base forms. They are like the word "to" in English. For example, you say "to eat," where "eat" is the verb and "to" is the infinitive.

That means that "hablar" is not just translated as "speak" but it is correctly translated as "to speak." In the same token, "vivir" should not just be translated into "live" but it should be translated as "to live."

Conjugating Verbs

You will have to conjugate verbs when used with nouns and pronouns. Let's take "hablar" (to speak) as an example. We can use this verb with the following pronouns: they, we, she, he, you, as well as I.

From "hablar," you can conjugate the word using the following:

>I speak = *yo hablo*
>
>you speak = *usted habla*
>
>we speak = *nosotros hablamos* or you can say **as hablamos**
>
>you-all speak = *ustedes hablan*

From "vivir" (to live), you can conjugate it by doing the following:

>I live = *yo vivo*
>
>you live = *usted vive*
>
>we live = *nosotros vivimos* or you can say **as *vivimos***
>
>you-all live = *ustedes viven*

From the above examples we can deduce that in order to conjugate a verb with "yo" you have to drop the ending of a verb and then you add an "-o" at the end.

For example:

- "hablar" ends in "ar" so you drop that and then you add "-o" then you come up with "hablo"

If you're trying to say "you" formally you conjugate the verb by dropping the last syllable and then you either add an "e" or an "a." However, if you're dealing a verb ending in "ar" then just add an "a." If you're dealing with a verb that ends in an "ir" or one that ends in an "er" then just add an "e."

Consider our previous examples:

- "vivir" ends in "ir" which you will drop. You will then replace it with an "e." Thus you end up with "vive"

- "comer" take away "er" and then replace it with an "e" then you get "come"

- To conjugate "hablar" take away "ar" and replace it with "a" and you get "habla"

So, in these examples, we say the following:

usted vive

usted come

usted habla

In case the subject of the verb ends in "os" or "as" then you will have to drop the ending syllable of the verb and add imos, emos, or amos. If you have an "ar" verb then you should add "amos" to it. If you have an "er" verb then you must add an "emos" to it. If you have an "ir" verb you conjugate it by adding an "imos" after dropping the end. Consider the following examples:

> *Nosotros comemos* is formed by dropping the "er" from comer and then adding "emos."
>
> *Nosotras vivimos* is formed by dropping the "ir" from vivir and then adding "imos" thus you come up with the verb vivimos.
>
> *Nosotros hablamos* is formed by taking away the "ar" from hablar and then adding "amos" to make hablamos.

If your subject is ustedes, you will conjugate the verb by adding either "en" or "an" at the end. You will conjugate with "an" if the verb is an "ar" verb. You will conjugate with an "en" if you are working with an "ir" or "er" verb. Let's go back to the examples that we have been using thus far:

> The phrase **ustedes viven** is formed by removing "ir" from vivir and then add "en" to make viven.
>
> The phrase **ustedes comen** are formed by taking away "er" from comer and then adding "en" to make *comen*.
>
> The phrase **ustedes hablan** is formed by removing "ar" from hablar and then replacing it with "an" to make hablan.

Present Indicative Tense

Take note that the present indicative tense of a verb actually means several things. You will just have to figure it out according to its context. Let's use the same example already mentioned in this book to illustrate the different meanings this verb tense can convey.

Yo vivo en Mexico can mean the following:

    I am living in Mexico.

    I do live in Mexico.

    I live in Mexico.

Conclusion

Thank you again for downloading this book!

I hope this book was able to help you learn more about speaking Spanish!

The next step is to put this information to use, and begin learning Spanish from home! You will also need to learn more about the different parts of speech in Spanish to help you master the language. But take things one step at a time and make the entire experience a lot of fun!

Finally, if you enjoyed this book, please take the time to share your thoughts and post a review on Amazon. It'd be greatly appreciated!

Thank you and good luck!

www.ingramcontent.com/pod-product-compliance
Lightning Source LLC
LaVergne TN
LVHW021744060526
838200LV00052B/3460